ANCIENT MARINE LIFE

ICHTHYOSAURS

BY KATE MOENING
ILLUSTRATIONS BY MAT EDWARDS

BELLWETHER MEDIA • MINNEAPOLIS, MN

EPIC

EPIC BOOKS are no ordinary books. They burst with intense action, high-speed heroics, and shadows of the unknown. Are you ready for an Epic adventure?

This edition first published in 2023 by Bellwether Media, Inc.

No part of this publication may be reproduced in whole or in part without written permission of the publisher. For information regarding permission, write to Bellwether Media, Inc., Attention: Permissions Department, 6012 Blue Circle Drive, Minnetonka, MN 55343.

Library of Congress Cataloging-in-Publication Data

LC record for Ichthyosaurs available at: https://lccn.loc.gov/2022050381

Text copyright © 2023 by Bellwether Media, Inc. EPIC and associated logos are trademarks and/or registered trademarks of Bellwether Media, Inc.

Editor: Betsy Rathburn   Designer: Jeffrey Kollock

Printed in the United States of America, North Mankato, MN.

TABLE OF CONTENTS

WHAT WERE ICHTHYOSAURS?

PRONUNCIATION

ICK-thee-uh-SORE

Ichthyosaurs were ocean **reptiles**. They looked like dolphins!

Jurassic period

They first lived about 250 million years ago. This was during the **Mesozoic era**. They were most common in the **Triassic** and **Jurassic** periods.

5

Ichthyosaurs were the biggest ocean reptiles to ever live.

The largest were 85 feet (26 meters) long. They could weigh over 80,000 pounds (36,287 kilograms)!

ALL DIFFERENT SIZES

Ichthyosaurs came in all different sizes. The smallest were only about 2 feet (0.6 meters) long!

SIZE COMPARISON

about as long as three school buses

Ichthyosaurs had two fins on each side of their bodies. They used these to steer.

fins

tail

They also had strong tails. These helped them swim quickly through the water.

THE LIVES OF ICHTHYOSAURS

Ichthyosaurs likely traveled in groups.
They swam in the open ocean.
They dove deep to find **prey**.

They had **nostrils** on top of their heads.
They swam to the **surface** to breathe.

nostril

ONE BIG FAMILY

Scientists have found ichthyosaur fossils in groups. The fossils are pointed in the same direction. This could mean ichthyosaurs traveled together!

Ichthyosaurs used large eyes to find prey. Their long, pointed mouths were filled with sharp teeth.

Fish and squids were a big part of their diet. Large ichthyosaurs likely ate ocean reptiles.

ICHTHYOSAUR DIET

squids

fish

ocean reptiles

Large ichthyosaurs had few **predators.**
Their size protected them.

pliosaur

Big reptiles like pliosaurs hunted smaller ichthyosaurs. Ichthyosaurs used their powerful tails to swim away quickly.

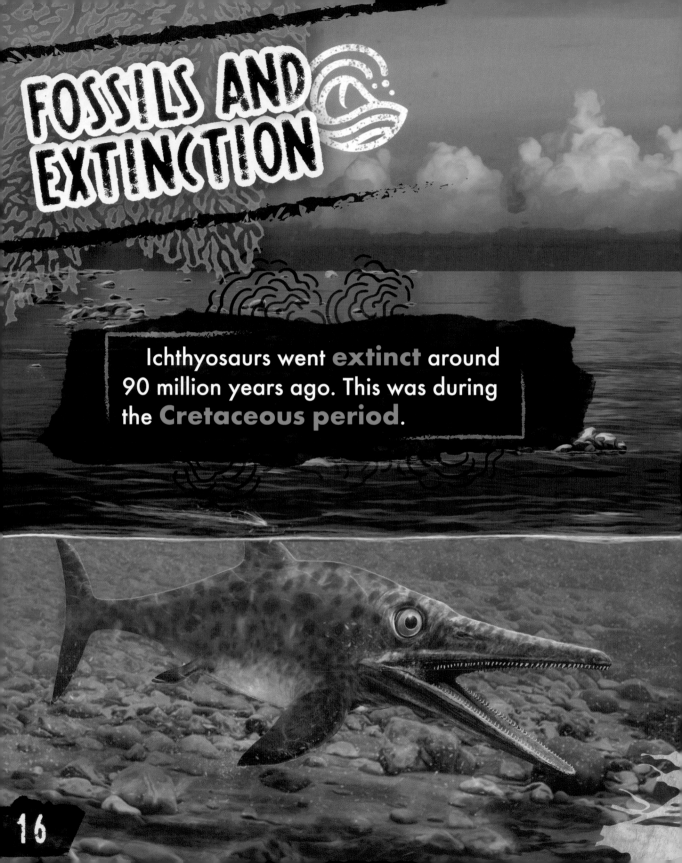

FOSSILS AND EXTINCTION

Ichthyosaurs went **extinct** around 90 million years ago. This was during the **Cretaceous period**.

Scientists are not sure why ichthyosaurs died out. They may not have had enough prey. They may have died from **climate change**.

The first ichthyosaur **fossil** was found in England in the early 1800s.

FOSSIL HUNTER

Mary Anning found the first complete ichthyosaur fossil. She was only 12 years old!

fossils

FIRST COMPLETE ICHTHYOSAUR FOSSIL FOUND

EUROPE

ichthyosaur fossil

FOUND in the early **1800s**

LOCATED Lyme Regis, England

Since then, fossils have been found on almost every **continent**. Ichthyosaurs swam all around the world!

GET TO KNOW THE ICHTHYOSAUR

WEIGHT
over 80,000 pounds
(36,287 kilograms)

strong tail

FOOD

squids

fish

reptiles

fins

SIZE up to 85 feet (26 meters) long

about 250 to 90 million years ago
during the Mesozoic era

Paleozoic		Mesozoic			Cenozoic
	Triassic	Jurassic	Cretaceous		

big eyes

FIRST COMPLETE
FOSSIL FOUND

in the early 1800s
by Mary Anning

LOCATION

every continent except Africa

GLOSSARY

climate change—long-term changes in Earth's weather patterns

continent—one of the seven major land areas on Earth

Cretaceous period—the last period of the Mesozoic era that occurred between 145 million and 66 million years ago

extinct—no longer living

fossil—the remains of a living thing that lived long ago

Jurassic—related to the middle period of the Mesozoic era that occurred between 200 million and 145 million years ago

Mesozoic era—a time in history that happened about 252 million to 66 million years ago; the first birds, mammals, and flowering plants appeared on Earth during the Mesozoic era.

nostrils—the openings of the nose

predators—animals that hunt other animals for food

prey—animals that are hunted by other animals for food

reptiles—cold-blooded animals that have backbones and lay eggs

surface—the upper layer of an area of water

Triassic—related to the first period of the Mesozoic era that occurred between 252 million and 200 million years ago

TO LEARN MORE

AT THE LIBRARY

Hamilton, S.L. *Sea Reptiles*. Minneapolis, Minn.: Abdo Publishing, 2018.

Moening, Kate. *Mosasaurs*. Minneapolis, Minn.: Bellwether Media, 2023.

Taylor, Charlotte. *Digging Up Sea Creature Fossils*. New York, N.Y.: Enslow Publishing, 2022.

ON THE WEB

FACTSURFER

Factsurfer.com gives you a safe, fun way to find more information.

1. Go to www.factsurfer.com.

2. Enter "ichthyosaurs" into the search box and click 🔍.

3. Select your book cover to see a list of related content.

INDEX

The images in this book are reproduced through the courtesy of: Mat Edwards, front cover, pp. 1, 2, 3, 4-5, 6-7, 8-9, 10-11, 12-13, 14-15, 16-17, 18-19, 20-21; Haplochromis/ Wikipedia, p. 19 (fossil); Sedgwick Museum/ Wikipedia, p. 21 (Mary Anning).